Letters

Barbara Thatcher

Presentation by *BookLeaf Publishing*

Web: www.bookleafpub.com

E-mail: info@bookleafpub.com

ISBN:9789358316056

First edition 2024

DEDICATION

This book is for you. The you I do or don't know but it doesn't matter. The you with a boundless mind and infinite imagination. The you that will read these words, take these symbols with a tenuous connection to meaning and make them into pictures and symbols of your own in your own way without any thought of me, invisible me.

ACKNOWLEDGEMENT

This book is for you.

Dear Cave,

369 Notareal St.
Iowa City, IA (abyss near there) 52245

September 30, 2023

Cave
Inside
The mind or possibly anywhere on a rocky
planet

Dear Cave,

Spelunk you the gray
That turns to blue black
and the darkness of a pupil

You make me blue
but the good kind.
I drip, drip, drip

Drip, drip

Drap

drip.

Covered in clothes and gear head to toe
but naked as a tomb.

Inside the inside
there is only down
and never out.

Crickets understand
what we never can.

The sound that bounces and spreads
the natural studio that dinah knew.

Wings felt in the face
A pinhole lit trail
a saving grace.

Footholds are false friends
and you are not for the faint of heart.

A challenge while touching your bony
insides
is to not think
about all the bodies
all the bodies.

Drip.

The bones of Australopithecus

a body not residing but dragged
in by a giant Eagle or some other
carnivorous monster.
no boogeyman required in the cave.

To wrap around me.
To provide a fantasy that the rocks will not
smash in on me.

Hold me tight
darker than night
and more threatening.
hold me tight.
in the rocks and catacombs
sway me in the subterranean rivers and lakes.
if I am not impaled in the heart then fill my
lungs with dark water.

Troglobitic are not we
but that doesn't stop us
for digging into things.

Rooting around the noise is close but distant.

Drip.
Drip.

a heartbeat.
a footstep.

a blink.
a drop.

freedom
inside the most enclosed thing.

taste it all around you.

Warmest regards,

Barbara

Dear Santa Claus or maybe Jesus or possibly Krishna, too,

369 Notareal St.
Iowa City, IA (abyss near there) 52245

October 1, 2023

Santa Claus or JC or Krishna
North Pole or Heaven or Goloka

Dear Santa Claus or maybe Jesus or possibly
Krishna, too,

I must admit I am a little embarrassed. I don't
usually do things like this. You don't usually do
things at all. What can I say? What can any of us
say? You've caused a lot of trouble. A lot.

I've decided I'd like a traditional Voodoo funeral.
I'd like a leprechaun and a Zeus to throw my
body off a boat.

My face may be red but not as red as you. Red
as your suit. Red as the pointless stigmata. Red
as a foot. Red as the sun. Red as the rage.

I wanted all kinds of goddamned things. I know
there were letters. They forced our pencils to
papers every year when the wind turned cold.
The cult they called school happily forced the
secular cult of big red down our gaping maws.

I was so tiny and the big con came in from all
sides. Godless motherfuckers ran the sting as
well. I knew they were all liars already but even
the dips that I believed would always be straight
with me. Those dips played me for a sucker. It
was the real big lie. I didn't go to any house of
worship weekly or even fucking annually so I
only heard about the crucified one when the
creeps that were blood crept in and dragged us to
that pointy house on a weekend or when
someone croaked.

I probably got some of those things, too. I
probably should not have wanted them at all.
Toys, maybe action figures of warrior girls.

No, it's the big lie. Getting what you want for the
annual spectacle of trash day isn't worth the
conspiracy of those, supposedly of age,

perpetuating an unhealthy myth of rewarding
good behavior and slavish obedience to the
nearest authority figure and fear of retribution if
your behavior is not good enough. I suppose
that's what being a dog is all about. I suppose
those are also my feelings regarding the afterlife.

Even if you are real, Santa, what's your deal?
Why the games? And Jesus, your shit is just
creepy.

Warmest regards,

Barbara

Dear Kitchen Window,

369 Notareal St.
Iowa City, IA (abyss near there) 52245

October 2, 2023

Kitchen Window
Kitchen
Anytown, USA

Pies sat in you.
They say it's true.
Some lattice affair
Stuffed with fleshy
Innards of ripe apples.

A showoff. Pornographic.
Created in that room,
Designed for unadulterated
Consumption and unconditional
Love. Inhaled and digested.

A pie-less kitchen window
Could be a translucent gate
A portal when eyed from the
Inside. The years tending

To the apron costume production.

Lighting the fires inside and
Hourly operation of the angriest
Of appliances ages. Through
You shines a carnival of possibility
Around that cage and that's the brightest.

Step out on the grass
And look inside you and things found
Are less like what you found on the
Outside. Knives and blood spatter
And third-degree burns.

Battered wives and crime scene tape
On the other side of that gate.
Dicks dusting for fingerprints,
Cutting the lights, and whipping
Out their luminol sticks.

Too much for you, Kitchen Window?
Something simple. An American
Shorthair. Some stripey affair
Drooping in you. An old man reads
At the wobbly oak table and eats pretzels.

Kitchen window, it matters not what you
Hide or your peepshow horrors.
Your existence in our caves echoes

In infinite options and the air that
Blows in that constant carousel.

Warmest regards,

Barbara

Dear Deers,

369 Notareal St.
Iowa City, IA (abyss near there) 52245

October 3, 2023

Deers
Pretty much any goddamn where I drive at night
and occasionally where I walk

Dear Deers,

For fucks sakes. You are everywhere! You are
cute and all but sometimes you're not. I've seen
some of y'all close up and yikes. Crusty and
tick-ridden, looking like the equivalent of a
gutter hobo but animal style.

People talk about authority over the night. They
say such as such does or does not own the night.
Well, of course no one owns the night. However,
you motherfuckers definitely are contenders. If
it's dark I am sure one of your ilk is running
amok without regard to any laws, even those of
physics.

And sometimes I need to remind you all that you don't own the night. I might scream out my window swerving around, delivering pizzas and cheesy breadsticks at 2 in the morning. You know who you are. A bevy I practically plowed over around a hairpin curve in the dense foggy wood on Linder Road. I swerved and almost biffed it down the dense woods. Fuck, I won't die running people their Domino's.

A rangale of you hanging out on the lawn in front of the garage that works on buses around midnight. When I made my right angle turn I had no choice but to roll down my window and scream out it to set you all straight. You don't own the night but you also clearly don't give 2 shits about me flailing at you as not one of you does more than a minor shrug in my direction.

But I've got an antler pick, too. I've seen your type of animal threat and be straight-up assholes. Snorting at me as I accidentally overtake you on an empty trail in a closed-down area of a state park. High as fuck, I think my sweaty autumn fear outweighed whatever baggage you had. I never plan to fuck with wildlife. Slowly back away I've done a lot but I'm still not that best at it. Like my sloppy slow back away when I was rambling around a few blocks from downtown and again almost overran a 5 pointer chomping grass under a tree on the fucking sidewalk. Always watch for a 5 pointer. I expect to see one in the shower the next time I trundle into a Best Western or any choice hotel to redeem some points.

Perhaps revenge for the night my mother hit two of you one night. I don't know the circumstances but I know it happened and none of us happy or proud and the Nova damages high. I have experienced as a driver and front door passenger a deer running into the car I rode in. Likely stirred up by hunters. I mean I know I can't relate to being tracked down for the purpose of becoming a trophy or the main ingredient in some tasty chili. I've never purposely caused any of your kind to perish and I am not even sure if I have had vehicularly. Maybe. The few times I've made contact with any of you, you kept moving, like lightning and disappeared into the night. I assume you ran and died in the brush. Maybe you cursed me in your last snorting breath.

A mob of you, possibly a family, traveled almost nightly to a large square field behind my apartment at the edge of the city near the river and park. I'd spy on you all in the height of the night. One time I saw a larger one straight up

kick a littler one in the head and the smaller one
winced away, giving the dickweed the tastier
patch of green. See, some of you are assholes.
Maybe not the fanged fantasies of some
Simpsons cartoon but possibly, if they were
human, they'd be a prick.

So, deers, let's make a deal. You don't destroy
any of my shitty cars or kill anyone I know or
me and I will slowly back away from you and
that, delicious chili.

Warmest regards,

Barbara

Dear Night Shadows,

369 Notareal St.
Iowa City, IA (abyss near there) 52245

October 19, 2023

Night Shadows
Night

Dear Night Shadows,

Darkness slithers on its belly
Snaking into the rooms and streets.
So many things and people it must meet.
Including its mate every evening, the
Shadows. Paired up in you.
The inky two of you invade, evade,
Handle the night. You leave your skin,
Shedding in corners and armoires
Edging the lampshades and street lights.
This reptilian duo dapples and distorts,
Makes ghouls out of hanging laundry and shoes.
Tears into our night time fantasies, turning
fingers
Into puppets, and twisting blankets into easy
nightmares,

Rich with shapeshifters limited only by
imaginations.
Your marriage of night and shadow born out of
dark and
Light.
Massacred quickly as to kill a snake is to cut off
its
Head, and to stop you would be to welcome the
pure dark.
The cleanest dark. The dark of lost extremities.
The dark that bleeds
Into my body. The other death is the slow death
of sunrise. Slicing out
The shadows like some slow torture, cutting
pieces until the pieces
Shine into the brown of day shadows and you're
laid to rest until
We meet again and you
Slither in at
Sunset.

Warmest regards,

Barbara

Dear Road,

369 Notareal St.
Iowa City, IA (abyss near there) 52245

October 4, 2023

Road
Wherever humans endeavored or managed to
beat too many paths but somehow felt that they
needed that access
Earth and I am not sure wherever else

Dear Road,

Constructed and worn.
Black, brown, gray, yellow, red.

Blue and rotten with travelers.
Rotten and gorgeous.
Bloated with twitching,
Writhing passengers and pilots

Coursing across the hotplate
Of the countries. Of the states. Plodding

Over potholes, cracks, and broken

you. The blaze never ends. The urge
To sail and soar to outdrive boredom,
To outdrive my soul, my body,

My control. Dear Road I love how
You do what you do when you do

What you do. You tunnel through
Tall mountains for me. You scream up
Hillsides for me. You ribbon the ocean
For me. You chop across the prairie. You

Bridge the continental divide. You line
The bridges of my known world. Without

These routes, lost and enslaved, imprisoned,
Clueless we'd be. Our trips and commutes
Derailed. Our quests and treks to new
Views and unknown perils cut short unlike

You. You are never short. Made of rocks, gravel,
gumption.
Made of desire and pain. Made of strife and
destination.

Warmest regards,

Barbara

Dear Bad People,

369 Notareal St.
Iowa City, IA (abyss near there) 52245

October 12, 2023

Bad Places
Any fucking where on this earth and possibly in
orbit

Dear Bad People,

That thought in bed,
In the dark morning and all the time.
Am I a bad person?
No character? No kindness?
Am I one of you? gooble goble gooble goble
Probably.
But I wasn't before, right?
I don't fucking know.
I am not sure.

Horse feathers and peacocks. Shoe leather and
combination locks.

Fuck, there are good people out there, right?

This isn't for you guys so there's a chance you
bad people don't know.

Cash registers and drowning captains. Mink fur
and dirty dish pans.

What's a bad person? In the eye of the beholder,
I guess. Some people kill. I don't do that. I've
done a lot of other shit religious books and
society and random people interviewed on the
street judge and label bad but haven't random
people, society, and biblical scholars done some
or all or more of those same things?

Flea circus and warfare. Baby fuss and dirty
pear.

What about killing in the name of blank? More
than a popular song, it's a sanctified way of life
for some but not myself. Are they one of you?
Are they bad, too? Am I more or less bad than
them? Where am I even going with this?

Lengthy ballads and ant farms. Caesar salads
and schoolmarms.

Are we born bad any fucking way? Do you bad
people feel it in your bones after the doc slaps
your ass? Do we come out heartless and cold?

Do we turn bad because of our upbringing?
Column A and column B? Is that possible? Do
bad people even know?

Dying tooth and frivolous lawsuits. Shell of a
phone booth and sabotaged parachute.

Bad people, this one is for you. I tell myself I
want to build character, control my reactions and
be good. This motherfucking thought in the
night. Fuck.

Bad people, I guess let me get back to you on
this subject.

Warmest regards,

Barbara

Dear Missing Women,

369 Notareal St.
Iowa City, IA (abyss near there) 52245

October 13, 2023

Missing Women
?

Dear Missing Women,

The multitude of different faces over the years.
Turned into thin air. You transform into the
gone.
In the wake of your absence, costly collateral
damage.
Living death embraces your children, your
parents,
Your lovers. Where are you and will you be
back?
Some bodies found and some never found. The
cruelest
Ghost of those whose fate is still unknown. No
milk carton.
No deck of cards, filled with your renderings
tethers you

Home. You vanished like a magician's queen of
hearts, slight of
Hand trick. One he can't cough up. You can
build a skyscraper of
Cards of your faces. They'd topple like the
memories when you
Fade from the media. The center of attention in
life or not that should center
Our attention in your loss as well. There Are too
many of you in the deck. Your
Lives and last known photographs subject to
time's indifference. Nothing
Left but maybe a poster, a fund, a name, a
cautionary tale, unlikely fame
For the lucky ones. At some point we measure
you in competition and victim
Blame. A junky hooker or a church mom all
deserve their equal shot. No matter the color.
Invisibility breeds amnesia and the missing see
the worst of it.
Missing women, I am sorry that we failed you.

Warmest regards,

Barbara

Dear Bee on the Flower,

369 Notareal St.
Iowa City, IA (abyss near there) 52245

October 14, 2023

Bee on the Flower
Wherever flowers bloom

Dear Bee on the Flower,

Like a damsel's handkerchief hovering before a
light sneeze
You hover and bounce around the lavender and
goldenrod.

Nature's show on display without shame and
admired
Now that we as a society decided we like bees.
We like you, now.

Watching this movie, the dramatic irony, ah, you
don't know
That you deposit what amounts to gold to us.

You keep feeding yourselves and in your flower
hopping
You feed us in your role and we can only hope to
keep you on the flower trail.

Warmest regards,

Barbara

Dear Gravel Pile,

369 Notareal St.
Iowa City, IA (abyss near there) 52245

October 15, 2023

Gravel Pile
Possibly in a pit or wherever gravel piles reside
in the world

Dear Gravel Pile,

Master of the calmest of states and the least
judgmental.

The pieces, separate, yet together, a
conglomeration, a pile.

A pile, all these pieces joined in union of
limestone, sandstone,

And basalt and other fragments of rock. You are
all the minerals

I need to get through my breakfast, lunch, and
dinner.

Oh crusher run, your simple stone beauty arrests me.

I'd follow you on Facebook. I'd follow you anywhere.

A blanket of fragments fragmenting into more fragments

That flows like a river and bends like a road. The rocks that crash

Like waves and give the gift of escape and meditation. To be you

Gravel pile would be an existence truly worthwhile. To break and run

Like you in a pile of pure power, of pure being in the moment.

Nameless and forever changing collaboration of loose and bonded

Earth.

Warmest regards,

Barbara

Dear Dreams of Paradise,

369 Notareal St.
Iowa City, IA (abyss near there) 52245

October 15, 2023

Dreams of Paradise
Somewhere in the gunk in between the ears
called my brain, 52245

Dear Dreams of Paradise,

A copy of a copy.
I have a bird's eye
View of it, in my mind's
Eye. It started as a child.

Some sort of personal
Soundless pastiche
Of clouds or an endless
Sky. Sure we all do.

I succumbed.
I never visualized
The fabled creature
That offered redemption

Including paradise in his hands.
Born and raised godless I still
Bought that bridge for sale of the
Ideal. Trotting out the usual tropes,

Clouds metamorphosed into the
Usual sandy beach with a sun, not hot
And searing but perfectly shining
At the right spot and the right temp.

Then absorbed into more lofty and responsible
The dreams became adult, meaning boring.
Dreams of peace. Dreams of no war and
equality.
Dreams not of pleasure but stasis.

Turned into the notion of nothing but sleep.
Sleep of the grave. Sleep of the ages.
Sleep so rich and dense you can eat it with a
knife.
Rapid eye movement so rapid and so mobile

It's more than a movement. Mostly my dreams
of you, elusive
Paradise involves taking flight. Riding that
rocket with passed away
Pets and orbiting Jupiter. Space, my personal
garden and riding
Around Saturn's rings.

No matter my dreams of you I know these
dreams are at best
A sedative to replace enumerating sheep
And at worst a common opiate everyone takes,
To cripple my life and standardize me in time
and space.

Warmest regards,

Barbara

Dear Future Self,

369 Notareal St.
Iowa City, IA (abyss near there) 52245

October 16, 2023

Me at 49 years later
? Perhaps kick ass space station or colony or in
some watery world

Dear Future Self,

I planned on typing up something for my past
self but I wouldn't know where to start. Instead I
decided to give my future self a shot.

Obviously you reside in a space station
retirement home. Be nice to your roommate. I
know you are quick to judge, to snap, and have a
low tolerance for discomfort so try to recall that
you are in space and have no place to get
quickly to and should be thankful and grateful
for life and a bed in space and all that stuff. You
don't know how bad your roommate had it on
whatever planet they exited. If they are in that

home, they live there for a reason. People make mistakes.

Try not to freak out about being in space and try to sleep. If you have any overlords, do your best to keep from working in the mines or some place else. Grin and bear it, if you can.

If you are on earth, it is obviously in a watery world type retirement home. Don't forget to keep up treading water and the same applies for your roommate here that it does in space.

Did you ever find that blouse you kept looking for? The one with the front tie. I hope so.

You don't by chance know of the scores of any major sporting events or lottery numbers a decade or so back?

Tell past me that you need to land on a date in the past to visit past me. I guess my issue is that so many times things have gone south, I wouldn't know how early to start warning myself of the staggering amount of bullshit on the horizon.

Hold onto that currency no matter what kind. Take that junk out of your mouth. Keep your

nose clean. Aliens and robots could be your
friends. I am not sure. Be patient and adaptable.

Warmest regards,

Barbara

Dear Alone Ones,

369 Notareal St.
Iowa City, IA (abyss near there) 52245

October 17, 2023

Alone Ones
All over in buildings, in bars, in theaters, in
restaurants, on the street, you know who you are
you glorious bastards

Dear Alone Ones,

Tribe of one and sometimes that's too many.

We are the ones, the ones, multiplicity in our
minds as our companions.

Grouped or coupled ones pebble us with absurd
questions.

We gaze at the navel without avail.

Bonded like gravel but we aren't alone together.
We are the alone alone.

Strutting on the inside, belonging to this group is
a luxury even the broke afford.

Bought by luck and self-entertainment.

Tears of the abandoned fall less when you see it
as the true success it is.

We alone ones spread our orbit and it is ours
alone.

The gorgeousness of empty seats surrounding
us.

The cocoon warmth of sitting singly at a table
surrounded by restaurant clang.

Ecstatically chuckling in a dark theater corner
with your popcorn bucket.

Every tick-tock of the clock owned by the alone
ones.

Any voice is your voice and it's only your
footfall on the stairs.

Quietude delights more than a sunset.

Freedom more far-reaching than the galaxies in
the universe.

Tribe of one.

Warmest regards,

Barbara

Dear Death,

369 Notareal St.
Iowa City, IA (abyss near there) 52245

October 18, 2023

Death
?

Dear Death,

We worship you. We celebrate you.
Oh the funerals. Oh.
Oh the arrangements. The spectacle of it all. The
true baller's ball.
Set me on fire without the ship. Shove coins up
my ass and a wreath on my head.

We fuck you. We suck you.
Whispering sweet nothings in a pretty portrait or
pulp fictions, we
Live to tongue your ear and taste you and be all
up in there.

We fight you. We shiver in our boots and piss
ourselves at you.

Soldier's statues and bombed-out quarters,
Mere crumbs of that pointless and endless battle.

We accept you. We see you.
In the grocery aisle shot in the heart like cupid's
arrow but lovelier.
Or in the hospital halls stinking of dirty adult
diapers.

You touch us lastly, unrolling your cloak and
pulling us inside.

Warmest regards,

Barbara

Dear Microsoft,

369 Notareal St.
Iowa City, IA (abyss near there) 52245

October 18, 2023

Microsoft
Darkest Depths of the Underworld

Dear Microsoft,

Can't you let me update when I want to? You force it or spring it on me. I swear you do. You are such a pushy creep and I realize I am typing this as I am using you to type this. You is a jerk.

And if I cave and update can you promise to not fuck shit up to the point of frustration, especially not at the exact moment I am taking a Teams call from my boss? Can you? Can you keep everything so I can find it? Am I asking too much for real, dickweed? I know I should be nice but the man hours I've lost on you.

Also, I am so tired of Microsoft Word Not Responding. I am not asking for perfection. I am asking to scroll down just once and not have you turn into a sloth on me.

In closing, please stop your dickish behavior so we can move forward in a more productive relationship and I don't have to feel enslaved to your quirks and glitches.

Warmest regards,

Barbara

Dear Blues,

369 Notareal St.
Iowa City, IA (abyss near there) 52245

October 19, 2023

The Blues and man, do they get bad
Wherever the pain comes from

Dear Blues,

You are a gas that shifts
From inert to active
At the drop of a job
Or a sunless winter night.

Always there and always ready.
Already through the door,
On standby to seep into my pores
Enter the bloodstream and paralyze.

You exhaust and tease and fill me to the brim
With mood swings. You and your sister anxiety
Terrorize and contort me. Chances are the
infections

Only just begun. Could be days or a decade.

A virus I battle and it's never clear,
If you just let me heal and I'll never know.
A lion tamer in the end leaves it up to the lion.
And you, blues, baby, you heal but the soul is
mauled

And poisoned. Every time, you leave another
Little piece of your poison
Prompting me to shriek, "where's the rest of
me?'
On the wind, a fugitive thief leaving that big
top-sized hole

In place of some vital part of me. The
transfusion uneven,
Without the proper prescription or sutures. Like
A duct taped gorilla suit and the best I can do is
barely
Make do. To want at least some of me to howl
through

The riddled suit. Blues, baby
it's what you do to me. Mixing metaphors won't
help.
No prevention and no cure
Means when it oozes under my skin, my best

Defense is none and chicken noodle soup
worthless.
To be less nervous than the knife thrower's
assistant.
To seize and jerk and dance with, not against
You my blues, my sideshow disease.

Warmest regards,

Barbara

Dear Muse,

369 Notareal St.
Iowa City, IA (abyss near there) 52245

October 20, 2023

Muse
?

Dear Muse,

Conjure you like Manfred on a mountain.
A witch with her coven in the woods.

As Goddess-y as you can get for me.
Not necessarily a daughter of Zeus.

The otherworldly. I don't know where you
Come from and where you go.

Rat like, squishing yourself through sewers
Eating shit and brawling other rats.

Foraging in the roots of a dead oak,
Hiding and hoarding shiny garbage.

Fleeing to a rotting warm basement
Busted washing machine in a lopsided house.

Muse, you'd never drag me to a grand ballroom
Or a Rolls Royce cruising amongst elegant
skyscrapers.

More like the backseat of a broke down Chevy
that's turned
Over or a dusty gas station with one working
pump and no bathroom.

Muse, whatever gutter or faulty elevator I
unearth you in,
I'd still stumble and stroll for a chance to bring
the gnawing again.

Warmest regards,

Barbara

Dear You,

369 Notareal St.
Iowa City, IA (abyss near there) 52245

October 20, 2023

You
You tell me

Dear You,

Thank you. You got this far and maybe you are still here. Maybe you skimmed and didn't read it but managed to come here and are reading this. Or you listened to it. Either way, thank you. It's for you. Also me, but you, and I am not you and I hope to thank you as best I can. I know a lot is out there, jostling for your attention. I appreciate whatever you've done. Whether you bought it or held it or read it. Thank you.

Danke.
Merci.
Gracias.
Spasibo.
Xie xie.

Thank you.

Warmest regards,
Barbara